A Long Way from Home

THE LOSS OF A LOVED ONE
AND THE JOURNEY THAT FOLLOWED

Christina Robin Resnover

ISBN-13: 9780578693392
Also available in eBook

Cover Artwork: Christopher J. Resnover
Cover Design and Book Design: The Author's Mentor,
www.TheAuthorsMentor.com

PUBLISHED IN THE UNITED STATES OF AMERICA

In Loving Memory of my mother and
grandmother

Gloria Marie Bryant – Resnover
(1957 – 2013)
Mariah Ann Resnover
(1927 – 2015)

Table of Contents

The Unknown 1

Grief 3

8 Months Later 6

Heaven Couldn't Wait for You 7

Time's Up...8

The Love You Should've Received 11

Crazy 13

Indiana State 13.............................. 14

Go Greyhounds............................. 16

College Dropout............................. 18

Stop Gaslighting Me 19

Mind Control 21

Too Late.......................................22

Growth 23

The First Cut is the Deepest 25

What's Good Enough for You?...................27

In Search of Everlasting Love 28

Was It Something I Said?.........................29

Endless Nights.............................. 31

Don't Dream It's Over 32

If These Scars Could Talk.........................34

The Good Ones Are Often Pushed Away 36

Tears I Could've Saved 38

Love Is.. 39

Remember Me 41

I Just Knew 42

December 20, 2015................................ 43

Keep It Real 45

The Breakup... 46

List of My Regrets.................................. 48

Heavier Days.. 49

Cover Us... 50

Self Love...51

Too Hard...52

When the Love Runs Out 53

Too Nice 54

People Pleasing.......................................55

Ex-Friends 56

Inseparable Us..57

Toxic... 58

The Giving Person 59

Fake Love 60

The Lost Ones 61

Misery 63

Glory Days 64

Summer 19" 65

"Dear Ma" 67

The Love You Gave 68

Faltering Faith 69

Goodbye Isn't Always Forever 70

Hello, Darkness 71

Be Encouraged...72

Acknowledgements 73

About the Author.......................................75

The Unknown

I'm not sure what's worse, to lose a parent at a young age and have no recollection of them, or to lose a parent as an adult and remember everything about them. It seems like either way the only guarantee is pain and uncertainty along the way. You don't know when it will stop hurting. Don't rush or push yourself to be over it even if you feel like you are. Grief comes in waves; one moment you could be happy or in high hopes, and the next minute you're crying in the middle of aisle of seven. Something you saw reminded you of them. It's okay to be sad and maybe even angry at times, just don't allow yourself to stand in the dark for too long. Don't beat yourself up over things you couldn't control or change. It's not your fault and it never was.

Grieving your loved one is a process, and no one can tell how you how you're going to handle it, especially those who haven't lost someone yet. Whoever you lost, nobody can tell you how you'll react or feel. They wouldn't know the pain of it until their time came. They will struggle to understand what you're going through and it's not their fault. They're trying, but sometimes their help is unneeded and not wanted. Not a soul should tell you when you need to be done grieving. Take your time and be kind to yourself along the way. You can't change the past, but you can certainly shape your future.

Surround yourself with loved ones and friends who will let you talk about the loved one you lost. They will let you openly be sad and cry about it if you need to.

1

Try to find a quiet or safe space where you can be by yourself and remember your loved one. Pray and cry about your loved one. Try to find things that will uplift you during your down times. Gather things that belonged to your loved one and have them in your safe space.

Know that you are not alone even when feel like you are. At first you may want to distance or isolate yourself from everyone; that will truly have you alone. Nobody wants to be *that* alone, especially during a sad time. Don't close yourself off, because it's you who will suffer more in the end.

Don't bring yourself more unnecessary pain and suffering. You can eventually let it go and that doesn't mean it stopped hurting. It just doesn't hurt as much as it first did. It doesn't mean you've forgotten your loved one, either. Your loved one is with you everywhere you go.

Grief

How can I still be me?
Trying to remain unchanged by something that I feel
has changed me
I can't go back to where it all went wrong and I can't
stop the inevitable from happening
How can I go back to my normal routine because now
nothing is normal about it?
I must now go on with a new routine
One that doesn't include you in it
I don't want it to be this way
Change makes my skin crawl
I feel sweaty just agonizing over it
I'm being forced to make a change
How can I move forward without forgetting who you
were to me?
The more time that passes the more I try to remember
everything
The harder I try to remember your face
Wishing I could hear you laugh
Wishing I could talk to you once more
Missing how you had all my favorite snacks after
school
I long to dance with you again all throughout the
house
The love you had for me I won't find it anywhere else
How can I maintain your legacy?
Hurting for what's to come
All the holidays, birthdays, and much more you will
miss
How can I move on?
Knowing our good times are gone forever?

The Day the Earth Stood Still

My 18th birthday had just passed. I couldn't wait for my first tattoo, days prior. You never wanted me to have tattoos. I would reason with you that they could be religious related, trying to convince you that tattoos didn't have to be a bad thing. My first tattoo was a cross that read, "God is Love." I was coming to the hospital to see you. Excited to show you my tattoo and tell you about the experience that I had. The excitement left the air just as quickly as it came. From the moment you said you had something to tell me, it felt as if someone had knocked the air out of my lungs. I could no longer breathe, drowning in a sea of tears on your chest. I knew it was going to be a long journey ahead and life would no longer be the same.

How could this happen to you?

You never smoked nor drank.

You never harmed anyone intentionally.

You didn't deserve to be sick, nor for it to be as advanced as it was. Weeks prior we went to the emergency room because you felt like you barely could breathe. The doctor told us you were fine, and he was rather rude. It was like our presence and concerns were a nuisance to him. For him to tell us you were fine and now weeks later you're in stage four cancer is abominable Your primary care doctor never suspected it either. He was your doctor for nearly twenty years; how was your cancer not diagnosed sooner? These doctors were supposed to take care of you, they were supposedly qualified. How did they allow your cancer to go undetected for years?

I wonder that some doctors don't care about the concerns of African American female patients. That their concerns aren't real, and neither is their pain. How many

4

African American women patients go unheard or unattended, too, that have passed away? How do we know that doctors aren't treating their patients differently because of their skin color or gender? Did they truly give their best, or the bare minimum?

How many African American women have been experimented on? If some doctors or hospitals would've cared a little more about health concerns rather than the color of your skin maybe, just maybe, you would still be alive. These lives matter just like everyone else's. Every patient should be treated the same, but we know this doesn't always happen. We don't know what's done in the dark until the truth comes out. The truth always comes out in the end.

Henrietta Lacks was a poor African American tobacco farmer. She developed cervical cancer sometime after the birth of her son. At this time, Johns Hopkins was one of the few hospitals who would treat poor African American patients. Doctors took samples of Henrietta Lack's cells without her consent. Her family had no knowledge of her samples being used in laboratories until twenty years later.

In 2013 at Indiana State University, I attended "The University Speakers Series," where two of Henrietta Lack's great-granddaughters spoke. That day was an eye opener; I learned the world of medicine took advantage of Henrietta Lacks and never asked permission to take samples of her cells nor use them for experimental research. It's unfair that Henrietta Lack's family had to put up a fight over trying to gain control of the HeLa strain. Had more hospitals been willing to treat African Americans, no matter their social class or money, would her cancer been detected sooner? Had she been treated elsewhere maybe doctors wouldn't have taken samples of her cells without her consent. We will never know, and we can't say, but we can hope this does not happen again to another African American woman simply seeking medical treatment and assistance.

8 Months Later

Watching you grow weary after your chemo is hard
Wanting to believe you can fight this
I know you can but at the same time, I know the odds are
        stacked against us
As I sit with you during one treatment after school
I wanted you to know that I'll always be by your side, Mom,
        that you're not alone

I watched you sob when you lost your hair
Your hair was your glory
Something you took pride in
Now taken from you
It seemed silly to me at the time
Hair is just hair
It will grow back
I thought about shaving my head to show you it's okay
Sometimes it's more than just hair

How could I expect to know what you're feeling?
Except for when you tell me I need to grow up
Telling me all your wishes for when your time is up
It's like you've given up
You're trying to prepare me
Stop telling me things I don't want to hear
You're not going to die
I don't want to lose you now
High school graduation is next month, and you're
        supposed to be there
I shut my door on you because I haven't given up just yet
I can't hear you talk this way
What you're saying can't be real
You're supposed to always be here

Heaven Couldn't Wait for You

I'm anxiously waiting for our Ambassador's meeting to end at school. I'm supposed to see you at the hospital today. You were admitted the day before and I didn't receive the chance to see you then. We start to head your way, and halfway there we received that fateful call. The hospital staff tried to resuscitate you, but you didn't make it. Now I'm sitting in the hospital parking lot sobbing. I called your baby sister to tell her the news, but I couldn't find my words. All I could do was cry on the phone. Suddenly, she's figured it out as she screams and cries on the phone until I hang up. I keep texting my Dad, but he isn't answering, and I need him now more than ever.

My world is shattered; I've never felt more lost.

I finally enter your room where you lie lifeless and I'm lying on you. Pleading with your lifeless body to wake up. If you would just wake up and open your eyes. Say something anything, Mom.

I leave the room to be by myself for a moment before everyone else arrives. I couldn't say goodbye, nor was I ready to, and I didn't see you alive for one last time. You died alone, Mom, and the worst part is, I don't know if you were in pain. You were worried about me right before you died, and we weren't together.

Maybe you felt like I was alone.

I know now you're no longer in pain. You love God and now you're with him.

Time's Up

I haven't missed school all senior year
The first year with no absences
It's been three days since you passed
I've missed school for three days now

All I can do is sleep on the couch buried in my sheets
My school is telling me I must come back already
Graduation is near and I can't miss anymore
It's been three days

And now I must try to pull myself together
What's the point when you feel so empty?
It's been three days

How can I grieve my Mother and finish school?
My school did their best to accommodate me during my
        rough time
But every minute of it was still painful
Like I'm constantly gasping for air
It's been three days

I receive all the sad looks at school
I know I look broken because I am
All my spark and light is suddenly so dim
Will this life ever end?
It's just been three days

Arrangements must be made for you
Your siblings want to bury you
Everyone's talking about what they want not what you
        wanted, Mom
You always voiced to me while you were alive your desire
        to be cremated

I knew nothing of cremation, skeptical to go through it
Cremation in the African American community is often
        seen as Taboo
I desperately don't want to cremate you
But your voice is clear: don't worry about burying you
I'm the one that must survive on and live
You said ashes to ashes, dust to dust
I will honor your wishes
None of your siblings came to your homegoing
Angry at me for not letting you be buried
It wasn't their decision to be made and it certainly wasn't
        their service
It's all right; I remember who was there and who wasn't
Your life was worth celebrating, not mourning
Yet, not many turned up due to the fact there would be no
        body at the service
It sounds sick that people rather see a dead body in a casket
To look and possibly gossip
I can hear them now: Did you see how Sister Gloria
        looked?
She didn't look the same
Did you see the outfit she was in?
That casket looks so cheap or, I could've bought a nice suit
        with the money that was spent
Such a waste of money and she's just going into the ground
All the lives you touched and people you knew
There's no reason why that church wasn't filled
This taught me something dear
Not everyone is your friend like they claim to be
Not everybody cares like they pretend to care
You were like the giving tree
Suddenly nothing left to give, and everyone fled away
It's just been three days

I endured much in those three days
I didn't know it back then that it wasn't meant to break me
It was for my good and not my bad
I was meant for so much more
This was just one of my tribulations
My time isn't up just yet

The Love You Should've Received

You never received the love you deserved
Your giving and loving heart too many
Seldomly returned to you
Still, your giving and loving heart to those in need
No one ever left your house empty-handed

Big or small there's something you've given
Sowing seeds everywhere you go
Your kindness greeting everyone
I never saw you mistreating anyone
You taught me to do things out of my heart
       and not for gain
Don't pay her, you say
I'm teaching her something, you said
Still resonates with me, Ma, and it always will

Thank you for teaching me to be kind even when it's less
       than deserved to some
To forgive those who have hurt me beyond repair
How God forgives us and tells us to forgive someone
       seventy times seven
To pray and remain faithful that God may one day change
       their hearts
As He is constantly changing ours as well

I've learned that it costs nothing to be kind
When someone asks me why I am so nice
I just say, it costs nothing to be kind
It's too easy to hate and stay angry
It's draining to be in constant madness and
       it's no way to live

We all should be kind to each other
To let go of those petty fights
To let go of moments that will cost a lifetime of affliction
      and distance
I'm not perfect and I slip up
But forgive me and pray for me
As I continue to pray for you
Let us love everyone and receive love in return

Crazy

It still hurts
They say I need to move on
Why don't you go seek therapy, they say
There's no one my age in these support groups
There's no one here that looks like me
Where are all the young people at?
Mostly, where all the young black people at?
Are they not hurting somewhere?
Mental health is still a stigma in the African American
       community
We tell someone we're seeing a therapist and somehow,
       we're seen as unstable
There must be something wrong with you
We don't receive the help we need and when we react from
       closing off so long, now we're crazy and unstable
As if they could understand my hurt and frustration
I wouldn't wish it on my enemy
An experience that changes you truly
Don't tell me it was her time
Yes, I know she's having the time of her life up there
But down here, she should be with me
The best mother God could've ever have given me
A pain so indescribable

Indiana State 13

First time away from home
Here at college it's not quite what I expected
Joined by many familiar faces from high school
So, I don't quite feel all alone
Yet, there's still an emptiness in me once everyone is gone
Wishing I could call you, Mom
To tell you about the classes I'm taking
Letting you know everything I've learned
All about the fun adventures I've had with my friends
Memories that will last a lifetime
I'm thankful for that first year it was everything and more
Thankful for this opportunity that I went to college and
        experienced dorm life
It's an experience everyone should have at least once to
        truly know what it feels like
All the new people I met along the way
The professors who were inspiring and the ones that you
        couldn't wait for their lecture to end
Struggling to stay awake in class after a night of last-minute
        studying
The nights spent in the library trying to finish up papers
        and assignments

Wishing you could visit me so I could show you around
        campus and introduce you to my friends
The ones that showed me a great deal of love before and
        after you left this earth
Everything was easier with you around, Mom
I'm growing up more and more every day without you
I know you would've been so proud

I can hear you now
"Don't bring me home no bad news
Bring me home something I can use
Go get your papers, something we can use"

It's been difficult, Mom, but I'm working on those papers
I'm working to be everything I can be
Never realized my true potential
That I was far more capable than I ever gave myself credit
I won't give up because you worked too hard for me to be
        anything less than great

Go Greyhounds

Second semester is finally over and I'll be transferring to
    the University of Indianapolis for the Fall
This is where life really kicked me, Mom
I made the mistake to transfer schools
I decided to live at home with Dad
Along with his wife and stepdaughter
All this to commute to school
Be closer to the boy I thought I loved
I say boy because he never was a man
A man is what I needed or so I thought

I believed that I needed to work and go to school
I'm an adult now and that means I should be working
To become part of the working class
My job was in the way of my studies
Spending time at work when I could be studying instead
My dying relationship in the way of my studies
I have no time to commit to you now and more so
    since I don't love you anymore

My desire to excel in math knowing it's never been a
    strength of mine
Trying so hard in class to understand
College is where the minute you understand one topic
    covered then by next class the Professor is onto
    the next new topic
How can I keep up in so little time without being
    completely lost?
Disappointment is what I felt as I watched my grades
    dwindle

I tried to receive extra help, Mom, I did
My professor couldn't believe how much I didn't
    understand
Was amazed how I even ended up in his class
The real kicker was I understood more math in his class
    than I ever did in any other math class
After this meeting with him I became discouraged
I was fooling myself; how could I ever move forward?

Not sure what more I can do I'm stuck between a rock and
    a hard place
There was no one to really blame; I was failing and had
    given up on myself

College Dropout

All I can think of is the scene from "Hamlet" where Hamlet talked about death after seeing Yorick's skull. Where he was trying to figure out the skull's identity if he was a politician, lawyer, and amongst other things. How no matter what power, status, or money you have it will amount to nothing after death. Is school worth it to me? It doesn't matter what life I lead or anyone else because once we die it's over. You can't take your money with you, degrees, or the power you allocated in your previous life. Can't I reach my dreams another way without accumulating debt? A piece of paper that's supposed to validate me but underpays me in this generation.

I would throw myself into endless and pointless jobs. The kind of jobs where you're nothing but a number, merely replaceable. Feeling unfulfilled and unaccomplished as I watched my friends continue at their colleges. Looking at their graduation pictures hoping to return one day. Some of my family and close friends tell me I won't go back to college. Even after I've stated that I know I will. It's hurtful because I expected their faith in me to be much more than what it was. I expected them to know I meant what I was saying. Yes, I know those who drop out or quit usually don't return. But when did I become one of those people and what about those who returned and finished?

We aren't the same and I've always done things in my own way in my own time. It would later turn out to be motivation for me to prove them wrong. I strive off people doubting me because they don't know me or what I'm capable of. I shouldn't feel the need to validate myself to anyone. God has validated me and that's the only opinion that should matter.

Stop Gaslighting Me

Everyone expects me to find my way
How can I look forward to the future when I'm not over
    the past?
Mourning for the old me and the past life I had?
I want things to go back the way they were
Can't they see the sorrow that lingers? And no I don't need
    your pity
No one is truly seeing me as I am
Picking me apart over my flaws
Picking apart what I wear
Picking apart how I wear my hair
Picking me apart over how I choose to spend my time
Ignoring their own faults and effortlessly pointing out
    mine
Choosing to misunderstand me than to hear me
I tell you that your words were hurtful, and you simply
    justify your actions
Now I'm the one who is overreacting, and I'm supposed
    to be immune like I don't hurt
They think they know me better than I know myself,
    awaiting my downfall
Constantly in competition with those not partaking
Stop overanalyzing me; I'm no one to study
You should worry more about what's going wrong in your
    own life than mine
How can you say you don't agree with whatever is going in
    my life?
Then I'm supposed to accept everything that you're doing
I don't match your guidelines, but you aren't walking a
    straight line either

I accept and overlook the wrongs and faults of loved ones
I love you as you are and in return, you can't do the same
I'm no one to blame; I was just trying to tell you how you
hurt me

Mind Control

You fill my mind with poison
Oh, the lies you speak into existence
Burning my ears with envy
Knowing I could never say such things
Your tongue spews out destruction
Why are you trying to bring me down?
Then love me as if it never happened
That's not love, love is kind
It's the people who misuse it
I forgive you endlessly
Manipulating me time and time again
Trying to break free of you
You think so highly of me until things end
That's when you say what you really mean
You become so disrespectful
A master in disguise you are
I thought you'd be kind, maybe just a little misunderstood
You were never the person I thought you to be
You aren't even an ounce of the person your friends and
       family think you are
When are you finally going to give up the gig?

Too Late

When did you realize you missed me?
Constantly, I'm the one to blame
Yet you yearn for the old me
In your absence, I found growth
Evolving into the mature me
I now know my worth, unlike those times before
Deserving so much better and I always did
Those times I settled for you feeling like I could do no
      better
The way you hate on women for not putting up with you
Boy, you're no man and you never were
How can you love when you merely lust woman, after
      woman?
I'll wait until I have everything that I deserve and
      unfortunately, that doesn't include you
So, it's too late to try and be friends
It's too late to try and make amends
It's too late because while I've forgiven you, I've moved on
This is a chapter I don't wish to revisit and keep reading
      over again
It was never my favorite chapter to begin with
This was a chapter I'd gladly end
This story must be written, and the focus was never you
This story still must go on after you
You were just a visitor
A lesson that needed to be learned
A mistake that must not be repeated
I don't hate you and I don't even dislike you
I just want to go on with my life and at one point I wanted
      you in it
I can admit that, but I want what it is meant for me
It's too late to rewrite this chapter

Growth

If you never make yourself uncomfortable then you'll
      never move forward
You can't keep looking back even if it's just one last time
One more time, far too many
Change is scary, but necessary
Scary is hard, but it's necessary
You can't go through life without change nor can you go
      all your life without feeling a little scared
If you're not scared, then the sky isn't the limit
Keep climbing until you're ready to make that leap to fly
Hold yourself accountable for all that you do as you do
      unto others
You can't walk around judging someone and chastise those
      who judge you
You can't sit around and criticize then feel offended when
      someone doesn't agree what you're critiquing on
When did you become God and sin free?
Suddenly you know everything and everyone else is wrong
Like there aren't times that you're wrong
Like there can't be times where you are wrong
Not saying I'm right, but I can admit when I'm wrong
I can at least say that I don't agree with what you're saying
That doesn't mean I'm trying to infringe upon your
      opinion either, because at least I can listen
How can we expect someone to go left every time if we
      always go right?
How dare we expect someone to do better and we don't
do it ourselves
How dare we say what someone hasn't done
I hope we're ready to tell everything we've been doing
What have you done to make a difference since you have
      so much to say?

How dare we tell someone to be kind when all we know is
        how to be mean
How dare you shut down a conversation without listening
        to what someone else has to say
How dare you be upset with someone for doing the same
        things you do to them
Why can't we all grow together?
Of course, it doesn't happen overnight
It's a daily process that we try and when we fail, we'll try
        again
Waking up each day still trying and thriving for the overall
        goal
How can we get there if we give up so soon
        not willing to hear what someone else may have to
        say or offer?

The First Cut is the Deepest

To the one that I'll always love
This one is for you, my dear love
I know what I feel is genuine, to me it's divine
Not what I was expecting blindsided from the start
I didn't like you because I didn't know you
You seemed like you could use someone to depend on
The sorrow on your face I resonate with
I know what it's like to feel alone and hurt
I could use someone I could count on
Could it be you, dear stranger?
You're the only one that I want to know everything about
     me
Closed off I am to everyone else around
They don't need to know me as I want you now
I don't seek to harm you or want anything from you
Only to love you, here I am

I can be myself with you around
If you could see what I see in you, or feel what I feel for
     you
Then you would know it's all real
No matter the time that passes, nor the people I meet, it's
     you the one I constantly seek
Searching for you everywhere I go
Wanting to love you proudly aloud and knowing the
     challenges that would come about
It's hard to decide which route to take when everyone tells
     me that I can't love you
That I can't be with you
I struggle to see how it's evil to love you
How can it be wrong when no one is being harmed?

Why can't we just be
You and I side by side
I lose myself in the thought of you
Here I am all renewed and collected again
I thought I knew life until I met you
I never knew what love was until you
Didn't think I could love anyone as much as you
No one can compete with you
This throne is reserved for you
No one dares sit in it knowing it belongs to you
I wait and wait for you to claim what's always been yours
Waiting for you to claim what you've been missing
Forever yours and more I am
Simply implore this throne made for you
I can't shake what I've been feeling
After all this time my feelings remain
After all this time I still want you
Will these feelings ever evade me?
Oh, this dilemma I constantly face over loving you

What's Good Enough for You?

I'm good enough to sleep with
Yet not enough to be yours
Yours and only yours
I'm more than a good time
Intimacy is a rarity
It's not for everyone
Sex is not just sex
It's something much more
A bond some may even call it a soul-tie
The mending and intertwining of two soul's energies into
      one
So much better when you're in love
Sorry not sorry, I'm reserved for those who are worthy
Worthy of my love and more
Reserved for those who can handle the essence of me
The one I know who won't count me out or add me to
      their count
I want an indestructible love and an undeniable bond that
      no one can question
A love you can stand on that will shatter rumors
There wouldn't be a shadow of doubt lingering in our
      minds to entertain such foolishness
I pray you find real love one day and that you love yourself
      more
Know that you're worthy of a love that can be reciprocated
      by the one meant for you
You are worthy of it and there's nothing wrong with you

In Search of Everlasting Love

I'm worthy of the love I desire
To love and be loved
Not asking for too much
To be heard without frustration
Held with compassion
Understood with respect
To leave without hesitation
When the love is no longer being served to uplift me
Speaking the truth where liars reside
I have nothing to hide

Take me as I know that I am flawed
Not claiming to be perfect, nor will I ever
Take me knowing I will make mistakes
I will mess up time and time again
But know I will love you on the hardest days and I expect
    the same
Know that I will love your family as if they're mine because
    they are
To know when you feel like you can't make it, I will hold
    your hand
We can get through it if we're in it together
That I could've chosen anyone, and I've chosen you
If we can't make it through the rain how can we make it
    through the hurricane
I need to see you at your lowest point to know we can make
    it through whatever
You need to see me at my lowest point to know I won't
    stay there either
If you can accept all of things maybe just maybe, we can be
    everlasting

Was It Something I Said?

Did I scare you off?
I was just saying how I felt
Maybe I wasn't clear the first hundred times
I feel you tugging at me by my jacket
Like you're trying to reel me
It's a certain closeness I feel when you do it
Then you stop like you're scared of what's next
I'm not sure what it is that you're scared of
Who are you scared of?
You hug me like it's the first time
Every hug is filled with love
There's not a hug you've given that was shy of perfection
The way you make me feel when your heart is near mine
Heart palpitations is what I feel
Be still heart 'fore I pass out
I rather not embarrass myself now

I tell you endlessly how I feel, and your silence fills the air
        each time
A silence I'm unknowing of
Is this not what you want
Say it for the world to hear
Say it for me to hear
Say it so it may be clear
Are we taking on the world together or apart?
It can't be both
I could just be your friend but it's not what I want
I want so much more, and I can't stop myself from wanting
        more
Each time that I'll try to be your friend, but my mind goes
        elsewhere
I'll be in your presence and suddenly I'm timid

The energy in the room shifts now I'm feeling like I can't
        breathe but I don't want to move
If I adjust myself, you'll see how uneasy I am
You make me uneasy and at ease all in the same breath
If I stay too still maybe, you'll think I'm frozen like I feel
        nothing
I can't turn to look at you when I feel your eyes from the
        back of me
Sometimes you act friendly towards me and other times
        not so friendly
Back and forth like the waves at the ocean not sure which
        direction they will go next

The older I become the more the uncertainty is
        unattractive
The uncertainty is all the time that has been passing and
        the no you're afraid to say
I should've said nothing and had you all guessing
Guessing all this time like you've been second-guessing
It's okay, I'm a big girl tell me the truth now 'fore time runs
        out
I won't be second-guessed by the next one that comes
along

Endless Nights

Just give me one night
Maybe my desire for you will end
Deep down this isn't what I want
If I can't truly have you
I'll say it's alright
I can put my feelings aside for one night
But I won't be satisfied for one night
For when morning comes, and your skin leaves mine
I'll be begging for another night
I'll accept whatever you have to offer
I'll give in and take less than what I deserve
I can handle not having more, is what I'll say
I'll lie just to be near you
Oh, can't we just lay here?
I want to touch you in a way you'll always remember
Your mind for the touching
Let me stimulate your mind
Open your mind up and let me take you on this escapade
I'll tell about what's all happened in my life from beginning
        to end
Where it all went wrong and what I did right
Trying to catch up for lost time
Trying to reconnect and hope in due time you'll be mine
Maybe you'll see me in a new light
Can we talk or are you just here for one night?

Don't Dream It's Over

Your eyes haunt me, constantly on me
Don't you know I can see you?
Aren't you tired of the façade?
Why are you so down ?
Don't you know I'm watching you, too?
I see you in my dreams, you and I
Your eyes on me
Don't wake me now, I'll enjoy this moment now
For when I'm awake again, you'll be gone
I'll realize none of it was real
It's scary how a dream can seem so surreal
The dream knows everything you feel. What you desire
       even though you feel it hasn't been on your mind
Your mind subconsciously still wants to remind you what
       you've been missing
A good dream is usually cut short as soon as it reaches the
       climax
Nightmares seem like they never want to end until you
       force yourself to wake up
Can't I dream about this non-existent life just a little more
It's not real but my mind is leading me to believe that it is
How rarely I dream of what brings me such joy
Rarely do I see this life I apparently want with you
I feel like it's my only way to be with you
I can be my true self with you around
Either way it's a catch-22
If I keep dreaming, I'll keep lying to myself
If I wake up, I may never have the same dream again and
       it still wasn't real
If this dream isn't real, then were you ever any definition
       of real to me

How can I separate this dream from reality?
Reality now seems so complex
Why won't I stop dreaming about you?
It's not all the time, just when I think I'm over you
I'll tell myself the same lie
I'm over you now
It's all just a beautiful lie

If These Scars Could Talk

Even though I know you're bad for me
I can't help but wonder where you are
What you're thinking about at this exact moment
I could never have ill feelings towards you after it's all said
      and done
Everything I felt was real and everything I said I meant
You're the only one I constantly remind that I love you and
      this much is true
If I could do it all over again
I still would've fallen for you
Not what I expected from the start
I couldn't have stopped myself from falling if I tried
Trying to catch myself endlessly and tirelessly
It always ends the same
They say time heals all wounds
Maybe time temporarily heals wounds
Some wounds may never heal
Even after the pain is gone the scar always remains
I can never truly heal and let the scar take its place
I'm rejecting something that is inevitable
The slightest thought of you I'm vulnerable and suddenly
      immersed with my love for you
A love that should go out but won't be kept out
A love that should be forgotten but won't be erased
You make me angry time and time again
I'm not sure why I do this to myself either
I can't help but to think about you anyway
Always on my mind yet still out of reach

I keep trying to outrun these feelings inside that eventually
       catch up
I know I can't have you but that doesn't stop me from
       thinking about it
We'll say goodbye again just as we said hello once more
It's better this way, I'll make myself walk away

The Good Ones Are Often Pushed Away

If you must break my heart just tell me to go
You won't let me in
The desire isn't great enough
Tell me the truth to silence my thoughts
Say you don't feel the same way
As I stand here holding onto nothing
So maybe I could stop going insane
Maybe you were always clear
My heart so clouded I couldn't even see
You were never the one for me
As I was never the one for you
I don't know you like I thought I did
There are so many different sides of you it seems
Struggling to find the real you just like I'm struggling to
        find the real me
The me I'm meant to be

Thought I would try and be a little more patient
I've been patient for years
When will I give up?
Thought I could be more loving
I've been loving for years
You give nothing in return
You don't care to know me like I know you
You'll say or do just enough to keep me wanting
But it will never be enough
I will never have you like I wanted
Maybe if I was someone different who didn't care and
        ignored you, your attention would be on me for
        once

That's not worth it to me for me to stoop so low
I don't need to change myself to be what you want
I have a good heart and if you don't want it, the loss is on
       you
I lost nothing but gained another lesson

People usually know what kind of person you are and what
       heart you possess
If they can't see it that's on them
It's not your job to make them see what they will miss out
       on
It's not being kind to yourself to have to tell people who
       you are and how you should be treated
It's not worth the pain and tears over someone who
       doesn't want you
It's okay because the one for you won't have a doubt in
       their mind about you

Tears I Could've Saved

It used to hurt me
For years, it hurt me
Those endless nights crying
Wondering what I could've possibly done wrong to you
        now
Feeling as if I'll never get over you
Trying to hold onto someone not meant for standing still
You're always on the go
I just want to stand in this moment with you
Can't you be still?
You were never the standing type
And you'd probably never will be
I can't run from place to place
I just want to find my place
When I find it, I'll know it, because I'll feel it
No longer questioning my place
I thought we could find our place together
Trying to force two mismatched puzzle pieces
Hoping one day that they might mend

Soon I'll receive the love I deserve
Next time it will be coming from me
Then I'll know who's right for me
By the way they love on me
Giving and receiving love in return
Perfectly imperfect we will be everything we need in each
        other

Love Is...

Why do we fight so hard for relationships that drained us
        the most?
I know I'm not perfect but some of you weren't the easiest
        to deal with either
Anyone who could've easily walked away from me didn't
        love me
If you claim you love me, this certainly must remain true,
        right?
Love is supposed to overcome and remain
You don't just wake up one day and decide you don't love
        someone anymore
If you can, then you never truly loved them
Love is even though you hurt me today I forgive you and
        we can work on tomorrow. No things won't go
        back to normal immediately. But if we're on the
        same page and working together then we're on our
        way.
Love is even though things have been hard lately doesn't
        mean we can't come back from it.
Love is, you lose it all today and I'll still love you
Anyone who cares about a relationship is willing to fight
        and preserve it. If they don't want to fight for it
        that's okay. Let them walk out on you. Let them
        make that mistake for themselves. Let them realize
        you will live on. It hurts immensely to end things
        when you want to save it, but it ended for a reason.
You didn't know it then but the saved you several more
        headaches and heartbreaks
How much more could you really take?
You cannot always expect a relationship be lovely

Disagreements arise and happen
Let's work on how we respond to each other
Talk to each other as if today is our very last day
If you cannot commit to anything why are you there in the
      first place?
If you cannot give God all of you, how can you ask Him
      to give His all to you?
If you cannot perform your job at satisfactory level, how
      can you expect raises and promotions?
If you cannot give your kids your all, why have them and
      not be there for them?
How can a farmer expect a Harvest with no crops?
Anything you care about you take care of
Don't claim to love something if you cannot fully cherish
      it
Anything worth having requires work and the commitment
      of it won't be easy

Remember Me

Never knew such love
A love not meant to be
Something that set me free
The love you found in me
From the moment it left your lips
I knew it was meant just for me
You saved yourself just for me
You were meant for me
Hello, fear
I have everything I want and need
Why are you here?
Hello, fear
You're wrong, I can save everything
I can save us
Hello, fear
Stop taking everything I love so dear away from me

I Just Knew

Never believed I could ever marry
The desire just wasn't fully there
It's hard when all you know is heartbreak after heartbreak
You start doubt the idea of love and finding it
But when I'm with you, suddenly everything feels right
I could easily spend the rest of my life you
It's crazy to think about
How could I know that I want to marry you and so soon?
Or am I not supposed to feel this way so soon?
I tell myself now, I don't think I'll ever get married
Doubting I'll find a heart like mine
But I'd choose you every time if I had it my way
I want to see your smiling face each morning as I wake up
        next to you
To tell you how much I love you and pray that you have a
        blessed day
One day we will find love again even if it's not with each
        other

December 20, 2015

Grandma, I cannot explain the pain I felt when you left
      this earth
Two years after Mother's passing
You were my last living grandparent
I'm now left with none
Everyone else is gone as well
I saw you at the hospital days prior to your passing
It's hard coming to hospitals since Mother's death
The smell in here is all too familiar with me
Feeling uneasy and anxious as I walk down the hallways
Hospitals are almost like a cemetery to me now
Right before I left, I told you that I love you
You simply replied I love you, too
That nearly broke my heart when you said it
To see you in the condition you were in
Yet you still knew it was me, your granddaughter
Oh, the love you had for me
I can't remember the next days that passed
But the one who my heart belonged to at the time who
      helped during this painful time
How you told me that you watched me sleep after my
      Grandma passed away
You wanted to make sure that I was sleeping alright
Oh, the love you had for me
No one besides my parents have watched me sleep
You were so good to me during this tough time and as you
      always were

Grandma please say Hi to Mom for me
Let her know that she's been on my mind
Let her know I'm slowly figuring it out
Let her know that I will see her again as I will you and
        everyone else waiting up there for the rest of us to
        join

Keep It Real

You no longer feel what I feel
Be kind enough to tell me
I anxiously can't hear your thoughts
Not knowing what you're trying to hide
Living life in despair
Pleasing and amending
When it's over you know
Be kind to yourself to let go
Kind enough so we both can move on
I no longer want to hold on
I feel you slipping away from me each time
I won't keep who doesn't want to be kept
I won't allow myself to feel so low over someone
You're not a prisoner here
Free yourself, fly on

The Breakup

I lost myself in grief
Crying so hard as if someone died
I couldn't explain the sadness that suddenly took over me
Barricaded in my room no longer going anywhere but work
Work seems to be my only escape from my mind
The only place where I'm not measuring every second and
        hour wondering what you're doing
Wondering who you could possibly be with
You were eagerly ready to move on
It's just to give you comfort and ease to be over me, you
        say
How can you say these things to me?
How can you be so ready to be in another's arms?
How can you be comfortable with knowing they're not
        me?
It's hard on certain days to get out of bed
Exasperating on the darker days that I occasionally fall in
I fall so hard I start to lose myself
The days where I could sleep all day and forget
Forget why I'm feeling this way
I'll just sleep it all away
It's hard to pretend like I'm okay with everything
It felt like you took everything from me and now my world
        so cold
You thought of yourself as you always do
You made it seem so easy to go
Burying myself in sorrow as I look at our old pictures
        together

You loved me and I loved you I don't understand
Somehow our love wasn't enough
You made up your mind
There's nothing else to be done
I can take comfort in what we had was real

List of My Regrets

I'm sorry for the times I didn't protect you when I
       should've spoken up for you
For those nights I pulled away from you
I should've been embracing you instead
Reassuring you of my love on the hard days
I'm sorry you had to question my feelings for you
All those times when my attention was elsewhere
You were a dream come true, everything and more
I couldn't possibly have ever thought to have asked for
       someone like you
How could I not have held on just a little more?

Heavier Days

Constantly feeling stuck in reverse
I take five steps forward and fall fifteen steps back
I feel like I'm trapped in a revolving door that never stops
Everything feels intense, like trying to anticipate the pain
      of ripping a Band-aid off
Nothing matters anymore and I don't matter anymore
I could fall off the face of this earth
It's better without me in it
I start to ignore the phone calls I've been getting
I could answer them but instead I'll let it ring
Slowly, not seeing my loved ones as I start to isolate myself
      again
Letting my job consume my life, it's all I do now
Surrounded by many, but feeling alone still somehow
Trying to cope anyway possible to fill the void
The stress in the moment feels like it's gone
Wanting that feeling to never fade
But eventually, I'm grounded again
Stuck in the same place
I never left and everything is rushing back up to the surface
I never truly dealt with any of it
Now I'm overwhelmed again wondering if this is it
To be better and do better
I must be willing to implement change and staying
      consistent
I must take control of my fear or live my life in constant
      fear

Cover Us

Lord, heal the brokenhearted
You are the only one who can mend them whole again
Remove the thoughts of suicide from their minds
They may feel like this the only way out when things aren't
        looking so great
They may smile day in and day out, but You know how
        their soul cries out
They know not their worth yet as You know all things
Walk with them for they are not surrounded in darkness
        when You are near, for You are the Light
They are blessed and have much meaning
They feel it not and know it not to be true
Their surroundings feel like constant reminders of
        disappointments and failures
Hear Your children's cries, surround them in Your grace
Give them the strength to carry on
For they are not alone with You near

Self Love

Why is it so hard to love myself
Yet so easy to love others?
To be there for them
When I can't even be there for myself
How can I claim to love you
When I can't love me?
I should be loving me
Catering to myself
Building myself up for when the world comes crashing
    down
I'll be strong enough to start over
I won't need to rely on anyone but God and myself

Too Hard

You say I love too hard
Maybe I could slow down
I say you love too little
You could give a little more
To be all in I certainly wish than to be barely in
You never were in it
There's no fun in not knowing you
It's uneasy for me to regard you in another way
To keep playing house without a future is surely a doubt
Why are you so afraid to feel?
There's no better way
How long can you be immune?
There's no one to fear here
No one here but yourself
You'll ruin the next big thing
You'll ruin everything it could've been
There's no going back with you
You'll keep running
You'll leave them all behind
One day you're sure to look up and find yourself alone

When the Love Runs Out

I've seen some couples make it and those who didn't
I often think about those failed marriages
The couples who didn't make it
Was their love not enough or was it easier to give up?
Can I make it with another? Can we make it?
Will our love be everlasting or is true love just a fairy tale?
That ugly word clouds my mind
To say it is like speaking it into existence
I long to be married one day
But my fear settles in
How will I know if I made the right choice?
Is such a risk all worth it?
Will you love me like I love you?
On the good and bad days for they're sure to come
Can we overcome, or become another statistic?

Too Nice

How can I be too nice?
As if there is something wrong with me
That maybe I'm pretending to be someone I'm not
Normal would be me cussing you out
Normal to you is screaming and yelling
You don't know how to react to nice
How to be around someone nice
Someone who respects you
Someone who acknowledges you
Recognizes with you and feels for you
I want to know you
Even the dark parts that you hide
It's like my kindness is a turn off to you
My rudeness would thrill you
You desire someone of disrespect
Someone who could bring you down then love you once
        more
Someone pretending to care about you and knowing it but
        expecting different anyway
They never had the right intentions for you to begin with
I'd always had the right intentions in mind
I'd be the one
I'll be too nice, not malice

People Pleasing

It's unfulfilling and life-draining
Diminishing one's worth
For another's comfort
Who is pleasing you?
Taking care of you?
It should be you
Constantly chasing those not chasing you back
Those who don't care about you, and therefore can't
    comprehend your worth
Stop letting people reach you
People will always be people
Leaving just as quickly as they entered your life, and yes,
    sometimes it hurts
Those meant to be there in the end will be
You won't have to please them they will be content within

Ex-Friends

After everything, all you could do was wish me hell
Despite everything I wished you well
Even if things had gotten so bad, I still had love for you
How could such a misunderstanding suddenly turn into a
        Revelation?
I thought so highly of you
You could almost do no wrong
You thought so little of me
So quick to think of me negatively
To think the absolute worst of me
I couldn't hurt you the same way
Tell whoever whatever you come up with
Lie on my name and say what I did
Don't bring up your wrongdoing
Put the blame all on me
Shout and curse my name
Lie to yourself and those around
You do this on the daily
Your curses cannot hurt me
Your doubts cannot weigh me down
You cannot catch me staying down
You cannot put your hands on me
No weapon shall rise against me
We were never the same

Inseparable Us

Thought we would always be friends
We've gone to almost every school together
You and I could never grow apart
Day after day we stayed in touch
You couldn't split us apart
Our kids will grow up together, we thought
They would become best friends as we were
Having our lives all mapped out
Who did we think we were?
Who knew things would be so different?
How things can change in a short course of time
Lives turned upside down
No longer seeing you around
I can't be the only one trying anymore
It's grown quite tiring
Your life goes on and so does mine
So long old friend
Until our paths cross again
If not, I wish you well, dear friend

Toxic

Those who dislike this word want to ignore the bad they
    may possibly harbor
It would force them to see in what ways they could be
    harmful to others
Accountability is a powerful thing, yet no one is eager to
    acknowledge one's own faults
It's much easier to cast the blame onto someone else, or to
    simply find fault in the word itself
Why does this word bother you so?
There are many words, yet many are tired of this one
Why can't people express themselves and talk about
    traumatic experiences as well as traumatic people?
We should call out toxic patterns and behaviors how else
    will we learn
If we cannot be honest with each other about bad
    behaviors possibly learned and passed on, how can
    we ever grow?
How can we call for change if we aren't ready to look
    ourselves in the mirror and talk in the same regard
    as we do others?
If you cannot face yourself in the mirror you have no right
    to deflect onto others

The Giving Person

They never cared about how their actions may affect you
        or how it could possibly hinder you
It was always what you could do for them even when you
        had nothing
They knew the kind of heart you had
You rarely said no, and it was always, how can I help?
They sit in front as you sit in the back
They see you as inferior, instead of setting boundaries,
        you've allowed them to walk on you
Now it's you never moving forward
It's you not going the distance like you always had
        imagined
Watching from the sidelines wondering when you'll make
        your break
They voted you out before you could even take flight on
        your own
They counted you out before they knew your life mattered
        and had meaning
Not knowing know the power you possessed and didn't
        expect to see you amount
Rise above the hate
Go ahead and show out

Fake Love

They claim their love for you when it was them loathing
     you all this time
Wanting you only to go so far
Not wanting you to outdo them when you supported them
They wanted you to limit yourself while they soar
Chasing their dreams while yours never mattered
They envy you secretly but aloud they won't admit it
Enemies masquerading as friends and family at times
Wanting to know your every move so they can counter
     block you
Never supporting you or showing up to your functions
Excuse after excuse makes it harder to trust
Those who can't support you were never for you
Friends can chase their dreams and support you, too
You can chase your dreams and support your friends
You should want everyone on your team to win
Don't let the naysayers fool you
Looks can be deceiving stand strong and press on through
Stay in search of the ones who love you for you

The Lost Ones

Why is that we never want the people who want us?
Is it because they will never amount to who we want?
Is it because we just want what we can't have?
It seems no one wants someone who is easily accessible
Some rather play a game or be hard to get
Some like the chase but if I must chase you around, will
       you ever let me catch you once I'm close enough?
Games are for children, we're far too grown
Then we can't have the people we want
Will we never amount to who they want?
Are we simply not on their radar, or maybe we're too easily
       accessible as well?
We rather chase the unknown of trying to win someone
       over who isn't seeking us out
Ignoring the people who could possibly be the better
       choice
We know that they're the better choice but still we don't
       care
How many times have we passed up our soulmates without
       knowing?
I feel like with two people when it's meant to be, there
       won't be any chasing
Everything will be effortless between the two of you and I
       mean, you won't have to try so hard
The right one will never have you guessing about their
       feelings for you
The right one won't leave you on read or send one-word
       replies
The right one will be fully engaged and immersed in
       conversation with you

61

Contrary to belief it doesn't take long to figure out if you
        want to be with someone or spend forever with
        them
You see couples who have been together for ten years and
        never marry
Then you see couples who have been together for six
        months and are ready to marry
Some say fools rush in but how many of them are actual
        fools?
Is it foolish to wait and wake up one day to find the one
you love gone?
What one won't appreciate in you another will adore what
        they like about you and even what they don't like
        because it wasn't the real deal breaker

Misery

Paycheck to paycheck
How can I save?
Paycheck to paycheck
How can I afford to live?
Paycheck to paycheck
How can I afford a family?
Paycheck to paycheck
How can I pay for my student loans?
Paycheck to paycheck
How can I pay for my degree that was supposed to secure
        me enough that I can repay?
Paycheck to paycheck
How can I find the experience needed for the job that all I
        thought I needed was my degree?
Paycheck to paycheck
This is no way to live from paycheck to paycheck
How can anyone live like this?
How can the wealthy stay wealthy and the poor stay poor?
Anyone can lose what they have today tomorrow
How can we overlook those in need?
Paycheck to paycheck
Those students dwindling in debt and expecting them to
        pay back six months after graduation
That isn't nearly enough time
How can you say they're ready when we're still figuring it
        all out?
Paycheck to paycheck must be put to an end

Glory Days

In such a rush to grow up
Not truly embracing such a gift given to us
Childhood is supposed to be the carefree part of your life
If we could go back to those simpler days
How come our parents never warned us
Would we have listened if they told us anyway?
One day you think you know it all
What kind of life you'll have and where you'll end up
Doesn't it occur to you that reality has different
        expectations for you?
God has different plans for you
When did you lose your inner child?
Enjoying life and chasing your dreams aimlessly
Growing up almost feels like you're losing yourself
One minute you're five then the next minute you're
        twenty-five, someone completely different
A stranger in the mirror
Honor that inner child sometimes
Would they be proud of who you are now?
Where you are now?
Do you see a disappointed younger you or a child beaming
        with glee?

Summer 19"

You lit up my world in such a short time
From the moment your eyes met mine
You waved to me like you knew me already
Your face emerged into this smile
I never knew another soul with such compassion like mine
Your loving heart healing my broken one
I tried to distance myself for as long as I could
You'd come plowing down every wall I put up
My silence didn't scare you off you welcomed it with hello
       anyway
Afraid of me, you're not angry or blissful, here you are
Every day we talked, and it was something I looked
       forward to
There's not a soul I talk to everyday
No one that's made me feel this way
The first night we hung out you hugged me like it was the
       first time you ever hugged anyone
You hugged me like you didn't want to let go
You hugged me with such warmth and love

You longed to see lightning bugs all summer
One night we sat in my car as the woods lit up
I was terrified of the unknown light abruptly
Lightning bugs appeared before us
Two weeks passed since you saw them last
One day I came over, and suddenly one flew by
You caught it to admire it right before you let it go freely
I felt as if our souls matched
You wanted to be around me as I wanted to be around you
Circumstances were in the way of us or maybe there was
       never really a us and there would never be

I was just a mere convenience in your season of doubt
I want to say you had me fooled but I'm not quite sure
I hadn't met someone as honest as you
I hope it all works out for you
Goodbye my lightning bug

"Dear Ma"

The day I graduated from high school and college, I felt
      nothing, Ma
To walk across that stage and see you nowhere in sight
The emptiness of a chair that was meant for you to be in
To cheer your baby girl on
It didn't make sense to have the desire to walk with my
      peers
But walking anyway for you
You were the one pushing me the hardest
You knew I could do anything I wanted
All the times you volunteered at my schools
You were always involved in whatever I was doing
It hurt, Ma, your existence no more
Left me in such a despair
I didn't see it coming
So many people coming and going
I'm tired of everyone around me leaving
I can't make them stay nor can I make them go
I know you're not here, but it doesn't stop me from still
      looking for you
Your teachings and guidance have not yet been forgotten
It was not for nothing
I'm going to make you proud ,Ma
This one's for you

The Love You Gave

When my world was coming down
You were my fortress of solitude
I felt safe near you
You and my Father are the only real I know
God, of course, above all
All of you hold me down no matter what
Some may not understand it
But it's not meant for them anyway
Surrounded by mean-spirited people
They have me questioning my own faith
I feel them trying to take my light
Turn me into something I'm not
I want to remain unchanged by this world
But there's no exception for anyone on this walk
I want to leave a legacy behind for my children
Praying, may their hearts stay pure
In these challenging times
May they grow old watching over their grandchildren
I don't want to change the world
I just want to do my part
I pray to God for His son Jesus Christ to save my soul day
        and night

Faltering Faith

I'm sorry, Lord, for the times my faith in You fell
During the darkest times of my life, I felt alone
You never left me
I was angry with You when my mother died
As if it was due to Your divine will
It didn't make sense for her to leave
For all these terrible things going wrong in my life
Easier to blame others than to admit to my own partaking
Running from the pain
You never left me
You made mountains move before me
How could I doubt You?
How could I not trust You?
You haven't failed me before
And You never will
You never left me
The Alpha and the Omega, You are
Surround me in Your grace
Reveal the steps You've ordered for me
I cannot outrun You
I cannot forge my own destiny
You knew who I was going to be from the moment I
        entered my mother's womb
Your way is the only way
And I cannot be without You

Goodbye Isn't Always Forever

It brings me to tears
Thinking of the future without you in it
Ma, I wanted you at my wedding, if I ever get married
I wanted to rebuild your house and do so much more for
      you
All my plans I had for you won't happen
You'll never meet your grandbabies who I've not yet had
You left this world without any
I know you wanted them
You'll never experience being a grandmother
When it's time for me to have children, I know I'll rejoice
      but without you here, at first will be difficult
I can't call you up for advice or have you over to watch
      them play
One day I'll have to answer my babies and their baby's
      questions about their grandmother/great-
      grandmother
I wanted my babies to know you
To feel and know the love you would've had for them
I wish they could've met the woman who gave me life
Maybe they're up there with you now waiting until their
      time will come
You're with them now taking care of them for me
You're telling them once they leave, they will have to wait
      for you again
Until we all meet again, Ma

Hello, Darkness

Your days are nearly over
Our time has been cut short
Those days I felt so weak
Those times I pulled away from everyone
Constantly sleeping
Praying to be whole again
The comfort of my sheets I wish to never leave
Hello, darkness
Who's this familiar stranger in the mirror?
Where has the old me gone?
From a caterpillar to a butterfly
I've been transforming
Letting go of the darkness before it consumes me
Stepping into the light that's meant for me
Hello, darkness, you've never known such a light
A light that cannot go out
Goodbye, darkness, you can't take my light
Goodbye, darkness, there's too much light

Be Encouraged

Dear reader, this book is for you struggling with the loss of
　　　someone
This journey is unlike any other one you'll go on
There will be days where the world feels like it's on top of
　　　you with no air to breathe
There will be days you wished could last forever
No matter where your destination is, and where you are in
　　　your journey, don't give up until you've reached it
This is for you who struggles with depression and suicidal
　　　thoughts
Who feels lost and overlooked
This is for you who doesn't feel loved
Know that you are loved, and someone values your life
If no one, God loves you and knows exactly who you are
Your life has meaning, and you are meant to be here
These poems are to let you know that you're not alone
This is for you struggling to find free grief support or
　　　someone to talk to
We must build foundations and organizations for those in
　　　need of support
Helping those in their time of grief because the last thing a
grieving person needs is another bill just to find someone
　　　to talk to about their pain
We must rally together and try to find some healing in each
　　　other

Acknowledgements

I want to thank all my family and friends who helped me on this journey to writing this book.

A special thanks to my father, Christopher J. Resnover, who took an idea I found and designed it into the cover art of this book. You've always been in my life and never neglected me. You've supported me in every way you can. I appreciate you more than you'll ever know. I love you, Dad.

Pastor George R. Blanks, founder of Perfecting Reconciliation Church International, in Bessemer, Alabama, I thank you for your advice and words of encouragement on the process of this book. I thank you for the time you took to speak with me and give me insight. As well as referring me to Ellen Sallas.

I want to thank Ellen Sallas and The Author's Mentor team for your time and effort spent.

Maurice Boston, I thank you for introducing me to Pastor George R. Blanks and helping pave the way for me to publish this book. You encouraged me to write all the books I can, and I will.

I would also like to thank Pastors Benjamin and Sally Thompson. During the time I visited your church, Progressive Life Ministries, I wasn't feeling like myself. I felt angry and was hurting around this time. It was Tim and Niko Glasper who told me about your church and invited me to stop by. I thank them for that because it was what I needed at that time. Your congregation was welcoming, and I felt so much love from all of you.

Sally Thompson, you gave me a journal to write down anything I felt or felt led to do. It was a few days later that I started writing down poems that came to me. I decided to turn those poems I wrote into a book. I'm not sure what led me to do it that day other than God. To use poetry as an outlet on what I was feeling and what I needed to let out.

I've always had a love for poetry. At first, I felt like I wasn't any good at poetry starting in eighth grade. I was struggling with an English assignment where we needed to write poems by the end of class. I thought at the time that all poetry needed to rhyme or be a certain way for it to be poetry. There are several styles and forms of poetry which are all beautiful.

First and foremost, I want to give God all the glory, honor, and praise. Without Him I wouldn't be here today. All the times I wanted to give up or end my life there was always more reasons to stay than go and I owe it all to Him.

About the Author

Born and raised in Indianapolis, Indiana, Christina Resnover is a graduate of Indiana State University with a Bachelor of Science in Philosophy. Christina's hobbies include playing video games, watching DC and Marvel movies, scouring flea markets for vintage comic books, and travelling. Her most recent trip was out of the country for the first time to London and Paris.

www.ingramcontent.com/pod-product-compliance
Lightning Source LLC
LaVergne TN
LVHW041206080426
835508LV00008B/818